JOSEPH PENNELL'S
Sketches
Of Old
NEW ORLEANS

E. C. MATTHEWS

HOPE PUBLICATIONS
P. O. Box 10062
Jefferson, Louisiana 70181

A. F. Laborde & Sons, Printers
New Orleans, Louisiana

RELICS OF THE SPANISH OCCUPATION

3

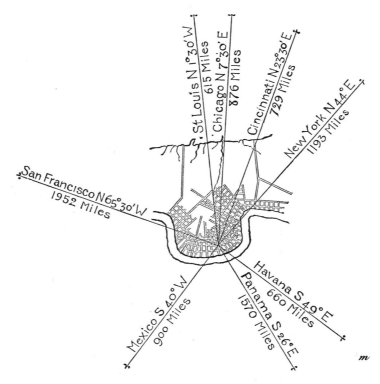

St. Louis N 1°30'W
615 Miles

Chicago N 7°30'E
876 Miles

Cincinnati N 25°30'E
729 Miles

New York N 44°E
1195 Miles

San Francisco N 65°30'W
1952 Miles

Mexico S 40°W
900 Miles

Havana S 49°E
660 Miles

Panama S 26°E
1570 Miles

LOCATION CHART, NEW ORLEANS, LA.

4

SKETCHES OF OLD NEW ORLEANS

The artist is able to see detail where others view things as a whole. He can lift from the mass a scene, a part of special beauty or importance and portray it to the world. Those were the things Jo Pennell did in New Orleans.

He was a tall, slim, young artist; mostly self-taught and here was his first important commission. Pennell received this order late in the fall of 1881, but could not escape jury duty and start at once. So he made sketches of his fellow jurors to fill in the tedious days before he could leave home for this great adventure.

In January, 1882, Joseph Pennell boarded a train South, from his native Philadelphia. He went to Memphis and then took a boat for New Orleans, so that he could make sketches of the boat's crew, roust-abouts, and other scenes on the big river. But the boat was slower than he expected and made too many stops.

Almost everyone on board played poker or enjoyed some other form of gambling. This became tedious for our artist as he didn't gamble, so he changed back to a train at Vicksburg, Mississippi.

After arriving in the Crescent City he spent that first night in the old St. Charles Hotel. They had a large lobby with men in large slouch hats sitting around in large chairs and surrounded by large spittoons.

The air was balmy that morning and Pennell enjoyed "the first real breakfast of his life" at Madame Antoine's.

As he described it -- when he turned off Canal Street into Rue Royale, he walked straight into Old France. That first day he moved to ground floor rooms in the Pontalba Apartments, facing Jackson Square. The landlady couldn't speak a word of English and Pennell had only a smattering of Philadelphia high school French, but they managed to understand each other.

INTERIOR OF AN OLD SPANISH HOUSE

7

After the chilly winter days up North, this warm sunshine cheered him through and through.   Pennell was a great admirer of the Spanish School of painters, especially the great Fortuny and Martin Rico.   Here he found the brilliant sunlight they had portrayed in such a striking manner.   Here he applied a somewhat similar technique to his etchings and pen drawings.

During the forty-four years that followed his New Orleans' adventure, Pennell went on to fame and fortune with his thousands of etchings, lithographs, pen drawings, charcoal renderings and paintings in oils or water colors.   But, in my opinion, none of those pictures surpassed his early drawings of Old New Orleans.

He sketched quite large, compared to the small prints we usually see of his work. These etchings and pen drawings were reproduced by woodcuts in Century Magazine during 1883 and were later forgotten by most people, or crowded out by his later work. Fortunately for us, the pictures were saved.   And New Orleans has saved most of those famous old buildings, while others were wrecking their landmarks to make way for new.

OLD SPANISH HOUSE ON BOURBON STREET

Pennell made forty etchings and pen drawings of Old New Orleans during the four glorious months he spent in this enchanting old metropolis. We are reproducing practically all of them; leaving out several portraits which would probably be of little interest.

Century Magazine paid him four hundred dollars for the illustrations and he paid his own expenses. Later, as a great artist, he often received more than that for a single picture. But dollars were very big over eighty years ago, especially in the South.

The artist picked his own locations or scenes and rendered them in his own way.

This was before photo engraving had been generally introduced and most drawings were printed from hand engraved woodcuts. Sometimes the wood engravers were a bit crude and artists were always complaining when the finer details of their drawings were spoiled in process of reproduction. Pennell had called some

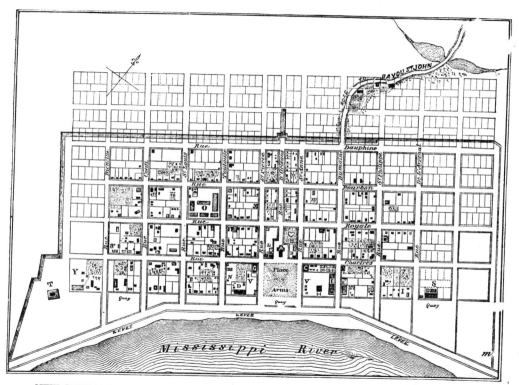

NEW ORLEANS UNDER THE FRENCH (ADAPTED FROM ORIGINALS OF 1728 AND 1761)

11

BIENVILLE

FOUNDER OF NEW ORLEANS · 1718

FROM THE RELIEF IN THE NEW ORLEANS CUSTOM-HOUSE

THE CATHEDRAL AND OLD PLACE D'ARMES, NEW ORLEANS

13

A FACADE

OLD CANAL ON DAUPHINE STREET (A RESTORATION)

15

of them "woodchoppers." But at the DeVinne Press, where Century Magazine was printed, they employed only the best engravers, and Pennell seldom had cause to complain about the reproduction of his pictures.

Most illustrations in those days were made very large compared to the little prints we saw in the magazines. They were photographed down to size of the printing block and then skillfully engraved by hand.

Our artist worked assiduously on his assignment but also found time to enjoy life in his carefree surroundings. He was popular with the ladies of New Orleans. Here he learned to drink wine and lost some of his other strict Quaker habits.

When he was sketching on location he usually bought a few fresh bananas for mid-day lunch and dreamed ahead to the good dinner at night, with wine and gay company.

Some of the Creoles did not like Northerners and one day Pennell asked a man to move so that he could get a better view of the scene he was sketching. The man

OLD VILLA ON BAYOU ST. JOHN

17

flared up, fixed him with his beady eyes and said, "I ham a Creole and you hair han American; for fifateen cents I will cut you into vera small pieces!" The artist moved away quickly to find a different viewpoint for his picture.

Pennell not only sketched but he visited with many characters in Vieux Carre: the priests and nuns, peddlers and "Queen of the Voodoos." The Queen would tell him nothing, but an astrologer told him, "You are serious, work hard and you will become a great man. You look like a scorpion, but faint at the sight of blood. Your wife will be your fortune."

18

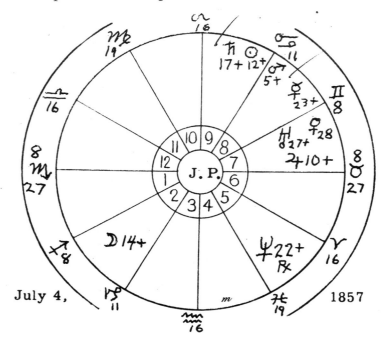

THE OLD CONVENT

His last note of New Orleans, when leaving for home, was Jefferson Davis on the wharf by the levee, seeing his daughter off for New York.

Over forty years later Mr. Pennell advised me to visit this "most interesting city in America," but it took me another thirty years, or until December, 1955, to get there.

Following Canal Street southeast, on that great white-way which points to the river, I discovered some narrow, old time streets leading to the left and turned off to enter a brightly lighted world of yester-year. Except for the electric lights one might guess that he was in "Gay Paree" of 1850. I had discovered Vieux Carre (The old square), pronounced vee ah car a. Tourists usually call it the French Quarter. This is the New Orleans of one hundred or two hundred years ago. These old streets, could they but speak, might many a tale unfold. This was Royal Street, the French called it Rue Royale and there were still a few signs bearing that name.

20

IN THE NEW CONVENT GARDEN

It was like something out of a fairy story; antique stores in old buildings, full of old furniture, cut glass, hand painted china, jewelry, guns, books, wonderful paintings and other objects too fabulous to describe. (At last I've found a place where the word fabulous really fits.) Then there were Belgian lace stores, perfume shops, restaurants and bars still carrying the atmosphere of by-gone days.

My first evening meal was eaten there in a brightly lighted old restaurant which had tile floors, high ceilings and cut glass chandeliers. Prices were reasonable and the people seemed more carefree than in any other large city I have visited. One raven-haired waitress stumbled and spilled a tray. "S.O.B." she yelled, with a French accent. Only she didn't abbreviate the expression, and even Harry S. Truman couldn't have put more feeling into that exclamation. Everyone laughed, including me. Then suddenly it dawned on me that this was the first swearing I had heard in almost two thousand miles of travel through the South. The Negroes did not swear on the streets down there, nor does anyone else. Up North they often

THE CABILDO OF 1792

23

use language in public that would have brought a blush of shame to the pirates and cut-throats who once walked the streets of New Orleans. (They pronounce it Nuorlans.) You can get along better here if you speak three languages and many of the stores had signs on the windows SE HABLA ESPAÑOL and ON PARLE FRANCAIS.

The next morning (Sunday) I was up early to visit Vieux Carre before the people were so thick. I walked the deserted streets, looked at buildings and read the many markers without interruption. It didn't take much imagination to see the streets peopled as they were a century or two ago. The buildings are still there, and the same old flagstone sidewalks, in many places, worn thin by two centuries of use.

Here was an old convent, built in 1734. (Said to be the oldest building in the Mississippi Valley.) The St. Louis Cathedral, built in 1749, the first "sky scraper" in New Orleans, built in 1774 at Royal and St. Peter. It was originally

24

THE CABILDO IN 1882 (THEN THE SUPREME COURT)

25

three floors and a fourth was added later. The corner of Royal and Conti was the financial center of the old city, with a bank on each corner. Two of the buildings were still there. The Louisiana Bank was opened in 1804.

When the Americans took over commerce was so heavy that the pirates had a heyday for a few years. The Lafitte brothers, Jean and Pierre, were among the most famous (or infamous) of these pirates. Between times the brothers operated a blacksmith shop at 900 Chartres Street. Nearby was the Cafe des Refuges, where the pirates, smugglers and European criminals gathered during the French and Spanish rule.

Jean Lafitte is said to have met Andrew Jackson in the Old Absinthe House, at 238 Burbon, to plan for the battle of New Orleans. The Lafitte brothers and their pirate crews were pardoned, for their help during this battle. In his later years Jean Lafitte went back to his old ways. He died in 1826. The house just mentioned bore a large white marble marker on the front enumerating their famous guests of by-gone days. It is like a list from the Hall of Fame.

THE GATE-WAY OF THE CABILDO

27

Another famous spot was the Cafe des Exiles, meeting place for the Royalists who managed to escape those wholesale executions of the French Revolution. Here is the one story stone house where Audubon lived from 1822 to near time of his death in 1851. (Famous artist known for his "Birds of America.") Then, the home of Adelina Patti, the golden voiced singer. Also the residence of General Beauregard, a confederate leader.

The old Spanish Cabildo, built in 1795, now a museum. Next, a cornerstone laid by Henry Clay in 1847. Places that entertained Thackeray, Marshal Ney, Lafayette, Zachary Taylor, Edwin Booth, Sarah Bernhardt, the Grand Duke Alexis of Russia, Mark Twain, Wm. McKinley, Theodore Roosevelt, Wm. H. Taft and many others.

Among the places I should mention are Jackson Square and the Napoleon House. The square, originally called La Place d'Armes, was laid out by Bienville, founder of New Orleans. It is famous for many historical receptions, including

28

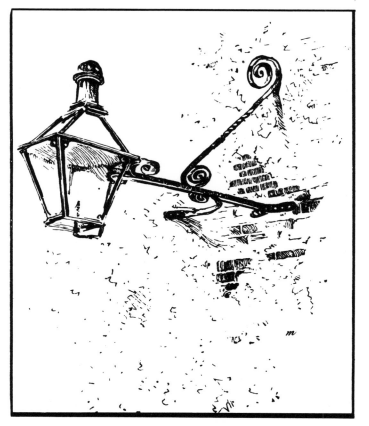

IN THE CABILDO

29

welcoming the Arcadians from Nova Scotia in 1755. (Perhaps you remember reading Longfellow's "Evangeline.") The Arcadians are the ancestors of the present day "Cajuns." The Napoleon House is a building of about fifty feet square, three stories and an attic with lookouts, located at Chartres and St. Louis. Girod, a very wealthy New Orleans merchant and former mayor, built this home for Napoleon. Dominique You and a gang of other ex-pirates were to rescue Napoleon from his place of exile and bring him to this home in America. But, before the plan could be carried out the "Little Corporal" died. The building still stands, among the hundreds of other historic old landmarks that space forbids me to describe.

The back yards, patios or courts they call them, are even more charming than the streets. And everywhere those porticos, balconies, fences and benches of beautifully designed "lace work in iron," scarcely any two alike. Most of this was imported from southern Spain.

IN THE CALABOOSE

The Vieux Carre impressed me so much that I still dream of the wonderful courts, the Pontalba buildings, Pirate's Alley and other unusual sights in Old New Orleans. Perhaps the people down there would say that I should tell you that Louisiana produces most of the cane sugar, molasses, etc. in the United States. Also rice, cotton, sulphur, carbon black and many other things. But those are mere statistics, which you can find anywhere.

The soil is rich around the delta, being the top soil washed down from all over the Mississippi valley. Perhaps some of it is from our old ranch in Colorado, and from almost a million other farms and ranches. They can, and do, raise everything.

Our old history books commented on Jefferson's great foresight in buying Louisiana territory for fifteen million dollars. Now the records in New Orleans tell a different story. Jefferson had no original intention of buying this vast territory. The trappers, traders and planters of Kentucky threatened to secede from

TRANSOM OVER DOOR-WAY OF PONTALBA BUILDING

33

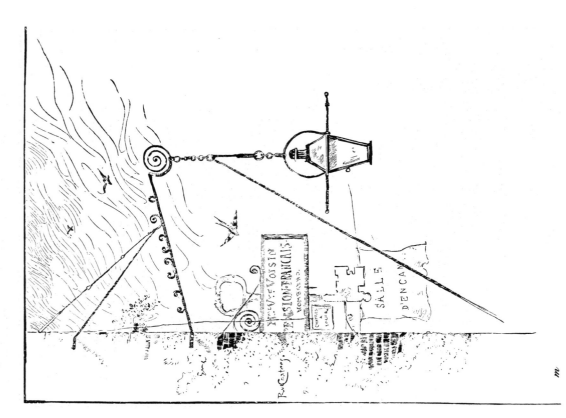

A CORNER

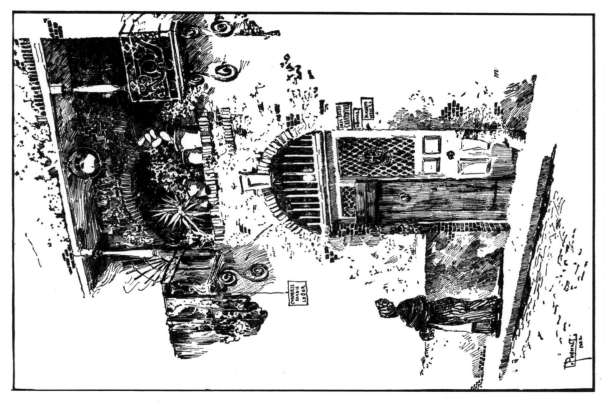

"GRATINGS, BALCONIES, AND LIME-WASHED STUCCO"

the union unless they were given free access to world markets through New Orleans. Jefferson sent Robert R. Livingston and a commission to France for the purpose of buying New Orleans. Tallyrand, French statesman and adviser to Napoleon said, and I quote, "Without New Orleans all of Western America is valueless to us." So the only way Jefferson could get this city was to buy the whole Province of Louisiana. Jefferson thought this would be unconstitutional without a special amendment. But so many people favored the purchase that he eventually agreed. The deal was finally consummated and this vast territory transferred to the United States in New Orleans. The mementos of this famous transaction are preserved in the old Cabildo there, including the table and pens used for signing those papers. After the deal was made Napoleon is supposed to have said, "I have given England a rival."

After the trip to New Orleans, Pennell went on to illustrate magazine articles for famous living authors of those times: Edward Eggleston, William Dean Howells, Henry James and many others.

THE MARIGNY HOUSE, WHERE LOUIS PHILLIPE STOPPED IN 1798

He spent over twenty years in Europe; made pictures of famous cathedrals and celebrated scenes that are too numerous to mention.

He was in close association with other famous artists; Whistler, Sargent, Abbey, and the ones best known at that time.

He was well acquainted with George Bernard Shaw, of about his own age and then quite unknown. G. B. S. was a good talker who seemed to be practicing elocution rather than talking for socialism. Both Shaw and Pennell enjoyed a good argument, so they found great sport in disagreement.

Halsey C. Ives, Chief of the Art Department for the St. Louis World's Fair, made trips to Europe and had Pennell help select the art work to be displayed.

Pennell came here to be at the fair and was on the jury to make awards. Then back to Europe for more years of illustration and art exhibits.

In 1912 he went to Panama to make his famous lithographs of the Canal; then made pictures of Yosemite and our Grand Canyon of the Colorado.

LUGGERS IN THE MISSISSIPPI

During World War I Pennell did a tremendous amount of work for the British and later for the United States, with great pictures of the ship yards, munition plants and other war time industries.

He visited the battle front in France but felt unable to do his best work there. He was a Quaker and believed in beating swords into plowshares. Some even accused him of being pro-German because he couldn't bring himself to portray the battle scenes -- besides some remarks he made about both sides being guilty.

By 1920 Pennell was back in Philadelphia and making frequent trips to New York. That year I went East in April to find a publisher for a book I had just written, remaining there until late in November. A mutual friend introduced me to the great artist and about my first remark was that he resembled my father in many ways. Mr. Pennell was quite a talker besides being one of the most prolific artists of our time. My remark that Dad resembled him, but was about the least talkative man I ever knew, brought the reply, "Just like my father, talk he never would."

40

THE OLD BASIN, CARONDELET

41

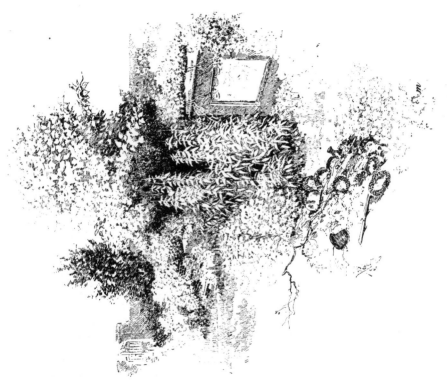

TOMB OF GOVERNOR CLAIBORNE'S FAMILY

A CEMETERY WALK (TOMBS AND "OVENS")

43

Pennell moved to Brooklyn soon after that. Then I was back in New York for the fall of 1925 and up into the winter of 1926. The same publisher was bringing out another art book of mine. We both lived near the waterfront, with a wonderful view of the Manhattan skyline, just across the river. Here we met many times.

Most people talked to Pennell about art, art, art! And though he was a most enthusiastic artist, I suspect he was sometimes bored with too much repetition of the same endless chatter. I was also a life-time art student, but our first talk had started off along different lines and later it was usually kept that way. We discovered so many agreements and coincidences in our lives that it became sort of a game, comparing notes to discover a new one when we met.

Mr. Pennell contributed a great deal of time to teaching etching and lithography at the Art Students League. He was given to caustic remarks about art critics, politicians, dusky servants, foreigners, prohibition and other "pet peeves." He had no time for "art geniuses." Like Edison, he seemed to think that real

44

IN RUE DU MAINE

45

genius was nine-tenths hard work. Most of the students loved him and took his criticism or sarcastic comments with good grace. He could refer to some student attempt as "a magnificent monument to mediocrity" and get away with it.

Between the time I saw him first and my second stay in New York, Mr. Pennell had been back to New Orleans; his first trip there since 1882. He was surprised and delighted to find the old city much the same as it was about forty years before. The buildings and places he had sketched were still there. He was so pleased with it all that he canceled part of a lecture tour to have a second visit in the Crescent City during that same trip.

Pennell gave art lectures all over the country and in Europe too. He belonged to so many societies and clubs, often as a functionary, that he was under considerable pressure most of the time. But that was the life he seemed to prefer.

Many of his talks were to women's clubs and they wanted him to talk about entertaining trifles, rather than art, so some of his audiences were a disappointment.
46

THE VILLERE PLANTATION HOUSE, HEAD-QUARTERS OF PACKENHAM

He said, "There is nothing like an old hen and the old American hen is the limit."
Some of these remarks did not go over well and he enjoyed considerable unpopularity in places. Even his native Philadelphia proved too much for him and a good illustration of that Biblical saying, "A prophet is not without honor, save in his own country."

J. P., as he sometimes signed himself, was a wonderful man, outspoken and honest as any Quaker. Sometimes he seemed to like those who disagreed with him better than those who would agree. It gave him a chance for argument. One thing I especially disagreed on was garlic. He loved it and to say I loathed the stuff would be putting it mildly. So I couldn't enjoy Mouquins, his favorite restaurant, in midtown Manhattan.

But we did enjoy comparing notes on our early struggles. His early life had been drab, little given to gayety. His parents made him wear Quaker garb and attend a Friend's School. Other children on the street taunted him by shouting,

48

OLD SPANISH COTTAGE IN ROYALE STREET, SCENE OF ANDREW JACKSON'S TRIAL

49

"Quaker, Quaker, how art thee and how's the neighbor next to thee?" Later the boys named him "Skinny" Pennell. While quite young he broke his right arm and then became left handed for life.

We had both always been scribbling pictures when we were boys and I must admit some of his early attempts were just as crude as my own. He broke his nose sleigh riding, while a school mate broke mine in a childish slugfest. I also broke an arm in early boyhood, but it happened to be the left one, so I never became a "southpaw."

However, I lived out West in the "Wilderness" where art was even in less demand than it was in Philadelphia during his boyhood. So J. P. went on to become one of America's great artists, while I became a sign painter (in order to eat regularly) in spite of my art interests.

His parents saw no future in an art career, so young Pennell went to work in a coal yard, but was allowed to attend night art classes. After I was a grown man

AMONG THE MARKETS

BEHIND THE FRENCH MARKET

THE OLD BANK IN TOULOUSE STREET

53

I worked for an ice and coal company in order to pay tuition and living expenses at Lockwood's Art School in Kalamazoo. Then fate and war times put a crimp in my art career.

Pennell and Dad were both slim and underweight, but with plenty of strength and energy. They had deep-set, pale, greenish-grey eyes, didn't care too much for haircuts, wore a similar moustache and beard and their features were a bit the same. Dad was born in January, 1857 and J. P. was born on July 4th that same year.

Many reference books give 1860 as his date of birth, but records prove the earlier date was correct. Some New Yorkers thought Pennell had "discounted a few years for good behavior," as people often do. But he was an honest man in every way and perhaps the date was forgotten, because people were always celebrating the country's birthday on that date and paid little attention to his.

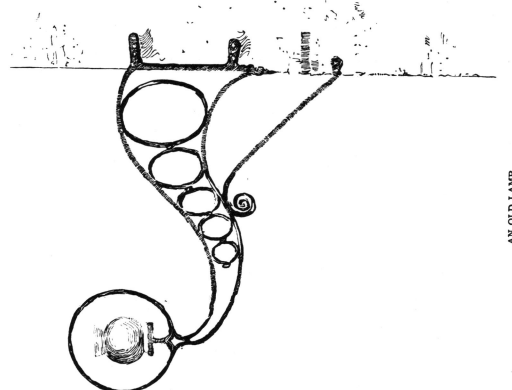

AN OLD LAMP

Mr. Pennell married Elizabeth Robins, a lady writer, in 1884. (The same year my parents were married.) He wrote many art books and she was no doubt a great help there; because the artist was sometimes a reckless speller. His father, a Quaker and a lover of peace, was very glad, at the time, to find that he was too old to be drafted for the Civil War. My Grandfather Matthews was born in 1812 and escaped it for the same reason. Both Pennell and my father had very vivid memories of that war between the states; although they were both young boys when it ended.

Perhaps Dad had amibitions to be an artist when he was a boy, although he never mentioned it. In fact, he seldom mentioned anything. But he became a self-taught surveyor and often placed small ornaments, such as a flag or a deer head, in the corner of maps that he drew.

In 1926 Mr. Pennell looked just about as old as my father did in 1956. Dad outlived the great artist by more than thirty-one years.

56

A FULL RIVER (LOWER FRONT CORNER OF THE OLD TOWN)

57

J. P. was sometimes driven almost to distraction by his multitudinous appointments, lectures and duties connected with many art organizations. He experienced many intervals of exhilaration or dark despair, depending on seemingly small trifles around him. He had no interest in sports and could only relax in his painting or in heated arguments with his friends.

Dad found time to go fishing, especially during his later years. And wasn't it Herbert Hoover who remarked that, in adding up your years the Lord doesn't count the time you spent fishing.

Pennell drank and smoked, but not to excess. In cartoons of himself he always made the big, black cigar an important feature of the picture. To him, liquor, whether wine, beer, whisky or what-not, was an essential. And he bitterly resented prohibition with the necessity of being a law breaker in order to live a decent, normal life.

58

THE "PICAYUNE TIER"

Liquor was plentiful in New York during the "roaring twenties" but the prices were high and the quality sometimes terrible. His favorite eating places went out of business, due to prohibition, and the world looked very dark to him at times. Often he longed for those good old days in New Orleans, where he could enjoy the brilliant sunshine, carefree surroundings, good food and anything he wanted to drink.

When the newspapers announced that Joseph Pennell had died, Friday, April 23, 1926, I was in Omaha on my way to the West Coast. What a shock it was, cutting one of the last ties to that golden age of American illustrators.

He was laid to rest in the Friend's Burial Ground in Germantown (a part of Philadelphia). His friends and students from New York and Philadelphia filled the little meeting house for those last simple rites. But I was too far away to attend the funeral of this great man, great artist and great friend -- just as he had been too far away when his mother died in 1882, while he was in Old New Orleans.

60

"The Dead Church"
4 mo 1882
New Orleans.

THE OLD BURIAL CHURCH

61

A CREVASSE (STORY'S PLANTATION, 1882)

THE BATTLE-GROUND

TABLE OF CONTENTS